UNIT 1
God's Gift of People

Parenting your 4-Year-Old

Dear Parent or Guardian,

We welcome you and your four-year-old child to Sadlier's *Discovering God's World.*

Know that you have our support and encouragement as you lead your child into a community experience of spiritual and social development. As the Catholic Church teaches, "Parents are 'by word and example. . . the first heralds of the faith with regard to their children'" (*Catechism of the Catholic Church,* 1656).

> "See what love the Father has bestowed on us that we may be called the children of God."
>
> *1 John 3:1*

How can parents fulfill their roles as "first heralds of the faith" for their children? They do this first of all by being good parents, the primary providers of nourishment, warmth, rest, and security for their children. This loving care is, for children, a concrete sign of God's love. In their everyday care and concern, parents also provide for needs beyond the physical. As the late Joseph Cardinal Bernardin stated in his book, *Growing in Wisdom, Age and Grace*, "While nurturing human values, such as security and trust, the parent at the same time lays the foundation for religious values, such as the love of God and dependence on God's care."

Supporting parents in laying such a foundation is the goal of this faith-development program for preschoolers. The aim of the program is to articulate and reinforce what is happening each day at home, where faith is spoken of and lived. As Cardinal Bernardin reminded us, "Formal programs of religious formation are important helps, yet they can only supplement the child's experience of living in a Christian home. Programs cannot replace parents in the religious formation of children."

May the grace of the Holy Spirit be with us as we begin this shared experience of faith.

The Sadlier Family

Additional Parenting Resources

Ames, Louise Bates and Frances L. Ilg. *Your Four-Year-Old: Wild and Wonderful.* New York: Dell Publishing Co., Inc., 1989.

Bernardin, Joseph Cardinal. *Growing in Wisdom, Age and Grace: A Guide for Parents in the Religious Education of Their Children.* New York: William H. Sadlier, 1997.

Leach, Penelope. *Your Baby and Child: From Birth to Age Five.* New York: Alfred A. Knopf, 1997.

At Home with Your Family

During the year, you will receive four of these special *Unit Pages* planned around the changing seasons of the year. These pages introduce the lesson themes in both their spiritual and social aspects.

The four *Unit Pages* will also offer you some insights into the normal developmental changes you can anticipate as your child grows and changes this year. A list of resources is included to help you further develop your parenting skills.

The goal of Unit 1, "God's Gift of People," is to help your child feel warmly welcomed within the preschool group. In preschool each child's self-esteem and emerging identity as God's own child is affirmed. At the same time each child is helped to develop the social skills necessary for making friends. Learning to cooperate in the group is also an important goal of the unit. These skills are at the heart of our growth in the Catholic faith as we follow Jesus' call to "love one another" (John 13:34).

In Unit 1, the children will explore ways to help others and to show their love. They will be encouraged to be caring and thoughtful of others in everyday situations. These loving attitudes are fundamental to Christian moral growth and development.

On each of these four *Unit Pages*, some children's storybooks that can further enhance the unit theme are suggested. These should be readily available at your public library. Sharing these stories is a wonderful way to spend time with your child while helping to extend and enrich the program topics.

For Storytime During Unit One

de Paola, Tomie. *Four Stories for Four Seasons.* New York: Simon & Schuster Children's Books, 1994.

Howe, James. Ill. by Ed Young. *I Wish I Were a Butterfly.* New York: Harcourt Brace & Company, 1994.

Wahl, Jan. Ill. by William Joyce. *Humphrey's Bear.* New York: Henry Holt and Company, 1989.

Wood, Audrey and Don Wood. *King Bidgood's in the Bathtub.* New York: Harcourt Brace and Company, 1985.

Lesson 8
The Sign of the Cross

We are all God's children.
God made us all.
God loves us all.

Here is a sign that you are loved by God.
It is called the cross.
Color or decorate your cross.

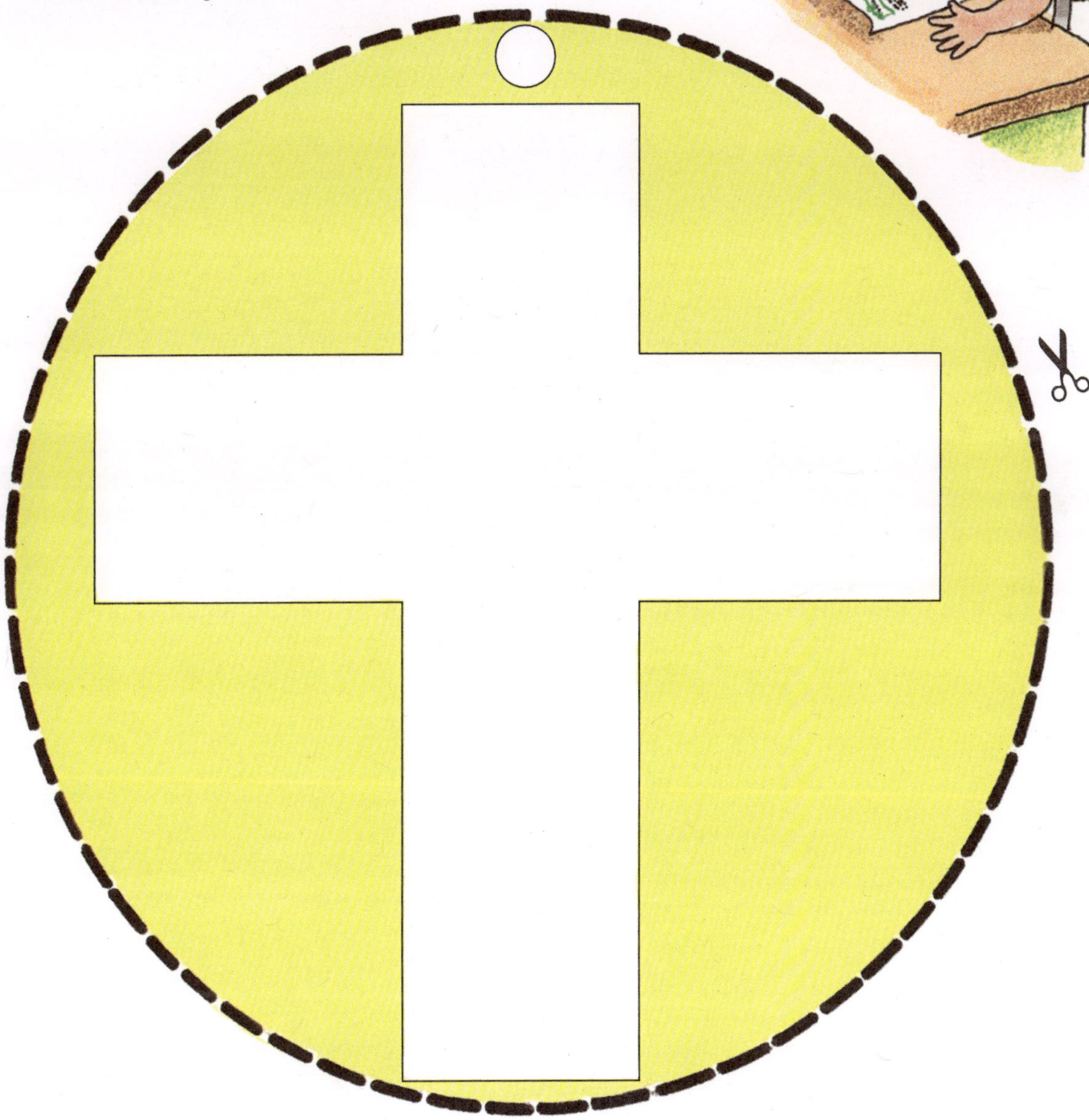

We belong to a special family,
the Church.
We are called Catholics.
We begin our prayers by making
the sign of the cross.

We pray.

In the name of the Father,
and of the Son,
and of the Holy Spirit. Amen.

Color the praying hands.
Cut out and wear your cross.

UNIT 2

God's Gift of Our World

Parenting your 4-Year-Old

The Young Child and the Sacred

One of the main joys and responsibilities of parenting is introducing the child to the world: first, to the world of the family, then to neighborhood, parish church, school, and, simultaneously, to the great wide world of God's creation and human achievement.

Initiation into God's life takes place in Baptism, Confirmation, and Eucharist. In Baptism, the first sacrament of initiation, with wonderful and profound ceremony, the child is given new life, the very life of God. This human child, with its heredity, geneology, personality, gifts, and vulnerabilities, is now God's child.

> Jesus said, "Whoever receives one child such as this in my name receives me."
>
> *Matthew 18:5*

Introducing this child of God to an awareness of the sacred is not as daunting as it might sound. After all, we know that we come from God and are going to God, and that we can find the sacred in everyday life if we only look. As Saint Catherine of Siena reminded us, "All the way to heaven is heaven."

How can parents point out this way to their children? Kathy Coffey, in her book *Experiencing God with Your Children*, writes that parents and children must seek God's goodness in each day:

"Julian of Norwich wrote, 'The fullness of joy is to behold God in everything.' Even small children can claim that joy: in dandelions and freckles, bear hugs and hot baths, warm bread and comfy sweatshirts. Children's five senses tingle with sensitivity. If after a tough day, the pizza drips fragrantly with mozzarella, the bedtime story delights, and the flannel sheets are warm, they find themselves embraced by God. Jaded people take these pleasures for granted. Saintly folks welcome them as coming from God's hand, brushed by the touch of the beloved."

Remind yourself often of the goodness of God. Then remind your children: "God is so good to us! He loves us very much!"

Additional Parenting Resources

Coffey, Kathy. *Experiencing God with Your Children.* Foreword by Dolores Curran. New York: The Crossroad Publishing Company, 1997.

Marrocco, Nancy. *Homemade Christians II: Growing in the Dark.* Winona, MN.: Saint Mary's Press, 1998.

Oppenheim, Joanne and Stephanie. *Best Toys, Books, Videos, and Software for Kids: 1998.* Rocklin, CA: Prima Publishing, 1997.

At Home with Your Family

The goal of Unit 2, "God's Gift of Our World," is to develop a sense of the sacred in your child as he or she discovers the wonders of the world God has created as a gift for us. Each lesson includes activities to heighten awareness of the various aspects of God's creation. Time will be set aside during the sessions to enable the children to contemplate the wonders of nature and to experience wonder and awe at the magnificence of creation. A simple reverent prayer, "Thank you, God" will be prayed by the children in response to God's gifts of love to us.

In each lesson your child will be helped to appreciate our role as stewards: that we are charged with caring for God's great gifts to us in creation. Are there experiences you can share at home that will enable your child to care for plants and animals or conserve water and help to keep our water supply clean?

The goal throughout the unit is to build on your four-year-old's natural sense of the sacred, and to explore with wonder and awe the elements of our created world—water, earth, plants, animals, fish, light, and darkness. Thanking God for these gifts will prepare your child to appreciate and to care for our beautiful earth.

For Storytime During Unit Two

Berger, Barbara. *Grandfather Twilight.* Putnam Publishing Group, 1988.

Berger, Barbara. *When the Sun Rose.* New York: Putnam Publishing Group, 1997.

Brown, Margaret Wise. *Goodnight Moon.* Ill. by Clement Hurd. New York: Harper Collins, 1991.

Bunting, Eve. *Ghost's Hour, Spook's Hour.* Ill. by Donald Carrick. New York: Houghton Mifflin Company, 1989.

Rice, Eve. *City Night.* Ill. by Peter Sis. New York: Greenwillow Books, 1987.

Ziefert, Harriet, and Andrea Baruffi. *Dark Night, Sleepy Night.* New York: Puffin Books, 1988.

Lesson 9

God's Gift of Water

What does water do for plants?
What does water do for animals?
What does water do for people?
Help the family find the ways
water helps us.

How can you help to save water?

Water helps plants and animals grow.
It helps us all feel clean and new again.
God made the water for us.
We will always need water.

Look at this picture.

Tell what is going to happen next.

How can you help keep our water clean?

We pray.

How wonderful you are, dear God.
Thank you for your gift of water. Amen.

Read to Me

Water is Everywhere

Where? Where is God's gift of water?
In the clouds
That float way up high
And bring the rains
That come from the sky.

Where? Where is God's gift of water?
In the streams
That flow slowly by;
In the lakes
Where the soft breezes sigh.

Where? Where is God's gift of water?
In the tears
That fall when we cry;
In the snow and rain
That gets in your eye.

Where? Where is God's gift of water?
In ice,
In rivers,
And don't forget the sea!
God made the water
For you and me!

Who gives us the gift of water?

Where do we find God's gift of water?

What do you like most about God's gift of water? Why?

Parenting your 4-Year-Old

Water Works

To a four-year-old, water is many things. Water is calmness: the calmness of a warm bath or of watching fish glide lazily in the family aquarium. Water is also excitement: the excitement of jumping in the waves at the beach or stomping through puddles during a spring shower.

As you have probably noticed, your four-year-old is wonderfully exuberant in the immediate experience of God's great gifts of nature. Water in any form is one of these great gifts. Give your child a tub of water, some toys and containers, and watch the joyful exploration unfold. (Remember, never leave a child unsupervised around water.)

> The Lord God said, "I will sprinkle clean water upon you."
>
> *Ezekiel 36:25*

Water play is not only enjoyable and soothing but educational as well. The words and concepts we take for granted (empty and full, light and heavy, small and big, too much, too little) are made real in the water tub. Perhaps you recall the story of Helen Keller and the life-changing breakthrough she made as she discovered the connection between the word W-A-T-E-R and the reality. In that connection, Helen, sightless from infancy, discovered the world. In a similar but less dramatic way, four-year-olds discover the world anew each day.

In time, the children will be taught the spiritual and sacramental meanings associated with water. The gift of water is integral to so much in our Catholic life: the sacrament of Baptism, the blessing with holy water, the stories of creation and of the flood, the baptism of Jesus followed by John's pointing Jesus out to all as "the Lamb of God." In his teaching, Jesus compared himself to the gift of water, a very powerful comparison in a desert country such as Israel: "Let anyone who thirsts come to me and drink" (John 7:37). Appreciation of these realities of faith begins with appreciating the reality of God's simple gift of fresh, clean water.

Remind your child often of God's goodness in giving us water. A glass of water on a hot day, a warm bath on a cold night, the splashing of feet in a playpool or at the edge of a vast ocean—all can prompt us to think of God. These are occasions to reflect aloud with your child: "God is so good to us! He gives us this wonderful water!"

At Home with Your Family

Building on your child's developing sense of the sacred, the purpose of Lesson 9 is to help your child discover the wonder of God's gift of water. The goal of this lesson has been to nurture a sense of wonder and awe and to help your child appreciate the greatness of this gift of water.

This lesson also began to establish the religious foundations for your child's later appreciation of water as a liturgical symbol. That water helps us feel clean and new again was explored as early learning for the sacrament of Baptism. You may wish to remind your child from time-to-time how good it feels when we have washed and feel fresh and new again.

Lesson 9 also provided experiences to help your child begin to take responsibility for caring for God's gifts of creation. Are there ways you can help your child learn to conserve water and protect our environment?

Enjoy the poem on the *Read to Me* page. Invite your child to tell you what he or she learned by using the illustrations on this page.

Finally, the children were introduced to a simple prayer praising and thanking God for the gift of water.

Discovering God's Gift of Water

You may wish to take your child on a water discovery walk after a heavy rainfall. Encourage him or her to listen to the water dripping from trees, drains, and so on. Smell the fresh air and water after the rain. Have your child look closely for raindrops on the flowers, puddles on the sidewalks, and so on. When you return home, let your child place ice cubes into large drinking glasses, pour cold water, and serve. How many wonderful ways we can enjoy water!

Water

(*To the tune of "London Bridge"*)

God made oceans, streams, and seas,
Streams and seas,
Streams and seas.
God made oceans, streams, and seas.
God, we thank you.

Lesson 10

God's Gifts of Earth and Plants

Make up a story to go with the pictures.
Draw what is going to happen next.

4

Seeds are planted in the earth.
The sun and water help the seeds grow.
Soon we have good food to eat.
Help the farmer find all the good things
from the earth hidden in the picture.
Color them.
God made the earth and plants.
They are God's gifts to us.

We pray.

How wonderful you are, dear God.
Thank you for your gifts of earth and plants. Amen.

Plants in the Earth

Tell me, how does a plant grow?

A farmer puts a tiny seed in the earth.
The sun shines on the seed to keep it warm.
The rain falls on the tiny seed.
Then, a tiny plant peeks out of the earth.
It grows taller and taller, taller and taller.

What is this plant? It is corn!
It is good to eat!

Thank you, God, for all the plants
you gave us for food.

Thank you, God, for all the plants
that are beautiful to look at!

We love all our plants.

Act out what happens to the seeds we plant in the earth.

What do plants need to grow?

Who gives us the earth?

Who gives us plants to grow for food?

Parenting your 4-Year-Old

For the Beauty of the Earth

In the beauty and abundant majesty of the earth, we see the mark of the creator's wonderful power. In the "dearest freshness deep down things" (in the words of Gerard Manley Hopkins) we experience the particular and unique love of the creator for all his creatures, even the smallest.

You may have noticed that your four-year-old is connected to the earth in a vital way. Fours are literally closer to the ground than adults. While this is a disadvantage at parades and in crowds, it is quite an advantage when exploring the "dearest freshness deep down things." Small crawling creatures, such as ants and bugs, are noticed and examined. Flowers and plants are met eye-to-eye. Even a rather modest pile of dirt is a mountain to a four-year-old, and must be conquered!

> "The earth is the LORD's and all it holds."
> *Psalm 24:1*

This enthusiasm for the natural world is both a means of learning and an invitation to discover God in everyday life. Creation is an ongoing message from God. The *Catechism* quotes Saint Bonaventure as he explains that God created all things "not to increase his glory, but to show it forth and communicate it" (293). In the beauty and abundance of creation, we can discern God's message of love and goodness.

In our own time, when so much of creation has been laid waste, polluted, cemented over, and despoiled by greed, we may need to discern and to pass along to our children another message of God's creation: stewardship. We must care for the great gift of earth that we have been given. The trees, plants, water systems, and animals have been put here for our use and care, not for our misuse or neglect.

Encourage your four-year-old to enjoy the earth. Give your child a shovel, a pail, and a digging spot in a shady corner of the yard. Or pour potting soil into a large plastic bucket (protect the kitchen floor with newspapers) and provide some old cooking pots and spoons to play with. Plant some seeds, indoors or out, and help them grow. Remember that, when he created the earth, "God saw how good it was" (Genesis 1:10).

At Home with Your Family

Lesson 10 continues to develop a sense of the sacred in your child by helping him or her discover that the earth God made for us is the source of our plants and our food. The children explored how plants grow from seeds planted in the earth. Sun and water help the seeds grow and soon plants are full-grown and sources of food for us. The children began to appreciate that God nourishes our bodies through gifts of the earth and plants, sun and water.

If your child has never watched a plant grow from seed, you might wish to enjoy this activity now with him or her. Be sure to help your child appreciate how necessary sun and water are for helping plants grow.

A visit to a farm is another way to help your child appreciate more fully that all the good things we have to eat are because of God's gifts to us and the hard work of our farmers.

In order to continue to encourage your child to respond prayerfully to God's great gifts, you may wish to repeat at home the simple prayer of praise and thanks to God that the children prayed with the group.

Taste and Name Good Food

Take your child on a visit to a farmer's market or the produce display section in your supermarket. Point out and name several of the fruits and vegetables. Explain which ones are vegetables and which ones are fruits. Explain how they are grown. Purchase some to take home with you. Examples: cucumbers, tomatoes, oranges, and grapefruits. Cut them open and have your child feel, smell, taste, and compare their likenesses and differences.

Growing Our Food

(*To the tune of "Mary Had a Little Lamb"*)

Now it's time to plant the seeds,
Plant the seeds,
Plant the seeds.
Now it's time to plant the seeds
In God's great gift of earth.

Lesson 11

God's Gifts of Birds and Fish

Look out the window.
What do you see? What do you hear?
Can you see the birds? Can you hear them sing?
Birds are a wonderful part of our world.
God made the birds for us.

How can you help take care of the birds?
Find all the birds.
Paste the star on your favorite bird.

God made the birds for us.

What does a fish look like?
What does a fish feel like?

Fish are God's gift to us.
God made the fish for us.
What do fish do for us?

Color all the fish in this lake.
Paste a star on the one you like best.

We pray.
How wonderful you are, dear God.
Thank you for your gifts
of birds and fish. Amen.

Read to Me

Look Around You

Here is a beautiful tree!
Point to the bird sitting on a branch.
Point to the bird feeding her babies.
Point to the singing bird.

Here is the ocean!
Point to the fish hiding by a rock.
Point to the whale jumping in the air.
Point to the school of fish.

Dear God, we love birds
that sing and fly.
We love the fish
that swim the seas.
We love your gifts.
How much you love us!

What do you like best about the birds God made for us?

What do you like best about the fish God made?

How can you help take care of the birds and the fish?

How can you thank God for birds and fish?

Parenting your 4-Year-Old

Cherishing Children

Preschool programs are designed and centered around the developmental needs and characteristics of young children. You have probably noticed that your child's preschool program consists of times set aside both for free play and for directed activities.

Play is the primary work of a child this age, as it is through play that skills needed for life are practiced: sharing, problem-solving, cooperation, and communication. These are first of all thinking skills that are put into action during play. Play alone and with others is absolutely necessary for mental and social development.

Jesus said, "Do not be afraid; you are worth more than many sparrows."
Matthew 10:31

Play is important for physical development as well. Young children's muscles, both large and small, are still developing. Running, jumping, skipping, and hopping help develop the large muscles, while working with play-dough, puzzles, scissors, and crayons develop the small muscles needed for grasping and, eventually, for writing.

Language abilities are growing rapidly. In preschool, circle time is an important time for sharing ideas, reading books together, and learning songs related to the topic of the day. You can encourage your child's fascination with words by reading from storybooks using repetitive rhyming sequences and nonsense words.

Many preschool programs include some formal academic work. It is best to approach this in an informal and light-hearted way. Concepts will be reviewed throughout the preschool years, so it is important to let your child develop at his or her own rate of speed. A non-pressured environment will help make a happy child.

A good preschool program cherishes children and affirms their worth each and every day. Teachers and administrators value the questions, interruptions, laughter, tears, problems, solutions, and possibilities that four-year-olds bring with them each day. Real learning, especially with fours, is always a joy.

At Home with Your Family

In Lesson 11, birds and fish were explored and appreciated as God's gifts to us. The children were encouraged to help take care of the birds around them. In what ways would this be possible where you live? Perhaps your child has never seen a live fish. Is there an aquarium you might visit near your home?

In the Scripture reference for this lesson, Jesus assures us, his followers, that we are of tremendous value. He first tells us that his Father's care extends even to the smallest creatures. He even knows when a sparrow falls from its nest. How much more, then, does the Father care for us, his sons and daughters!

As followers of Christ, we are charged with the responsibility of respecting and cherishing God's little ones, his children. This means that parents, especially the parents of preschoolers, find themselves continually offering explanations for the whys and wherefores of everyday life. If children are given simple reasons for rules and expectations, their problem-solving and reasoning skills will develop more quickly. The more they are engaged in their own process of human development, the more cooperative they will be and also less likely to "fall out of the nest." If children are treated with respect, they are more likely to treat others, and all creation, with the same respect.

Feeding Our Birds

Help your child to make several different kinds of bird feeders so that you can observe the birds up close. Place a couple of aluminum foil pans filled with birdseed on a window ledge or a table. You can also make a pine cone feeder by spooning a few teaspoons of solid shortening in the inside crevices of the cone. Roll in bird seed and hang from a low tree branch. Check often to see if refills are needed.

Praise God

(*To the tune of "The Mulberry Bush"*)

God made the birds to sing so sweet,
Sing so sweet, tweet, tweet, tweet.
God made the birds to sing so sweet.
We thank you, God. We praise you.

God made the fish to swim and splash,
Swim and splash, swim and splash.
God made the fish to swim and splash.
We thank you, God. We praise you.

Lesson 12
God's Gift of Animals

Some animals are so small.
Some animals are so big!
Name some small animals and
some large ones.
Some animals are wild and live
in the forest or the jungle.
Do you know any of their names?

Paste a star on the biggest animal.

God made all the animals.

Some animals give us food.
Some animals give us wool for warm clothes.
Some animals help us work.
Some animals play with us.
God made all the animals for us.

What do animals do for us? Match the pictures.
How can we help take care of the animals?

We pray.

How wonderful you are, dear God.
Thank you for your gift of animals.
Amen.

Read to Me

Can You Guess?

My name is Ellie.
I am big, strong, and gray.
My big flapping ears
Keep flies away.
Can you guess what I am?

My name is Leo.
I'm proud as can be.
I'm the biggest of cats.
I'm the king, you see!
Can you guess what I am?

My name is Jerry.
My long neck makes me tall.
I can munch on high leaves
Without stretching at all.
Can you guess what I am?

An elephant, a lion, a giraffe
We have met.
If you took one of them home,
Would it make a good pet?

Now look at this picture.
Do you see more?
Would you let one of these pets
Come through your door?

Parenting your 4-Year-Old

Animal Talk

Most four-year-olds love animals. If you take your child to the zoo, he or she will talk about each animal in great detail for days and days. However, owning an animal is quite different from visiting one at the zoo.

Unless you are willing to take full responsibility for the care and feeding of a pet, now may not be a good time to add a dog or cat to the family. Your four-year-old is not yet able to understand the dependence that an animal has on its owner for survival. Your child will enjoy helping with the care of a pet but he or she is still much too young for total responsibility.

> "Praise the LORD . . . .
> You animals wild and tame,
> you creatures that crawl
> and fly."
>
> *Psalm 148: 7, 10*

If an animal is already part of your family, you may want to invite your child to help care for it in some way. Preparing food or water, brushing it, or just playing appropriately with a pet are all ways to care.

Explain to your four-year-old that animals are creatures of God and need our kindness. Show your child the best way to pick up and hold the pet gently. Most animals are easily startled by the noisy and sudden movements of children. Remind your child to move slowly and quietly around animals unless the animal knows your child very well.

Sometimes your child may want to meet a strange dog, perhaps in the park or on a walk. Always ask permission of the owner before petting a strange dog, even if the dog seems friendly.

At Home with Your Family

The unit goal of helping your child discover the wonders of God's gifts of creation was continued in this lesson as animals were discussed. The children learned that the animals God made can be small or large and live in very different environments all over the world. Some of the ways animals help make our world better for us were explored. Invite your child to tell you about the matching game completed in the group.

Fours, so inquisitive about and delighted by new things they are discovering in their world, are at a perfect age for their first visit to a zoo or aquarium. Is it possible for you to plan such a trip? It is best to limit your visit to one or two hours at the most.

You are sure to be amazed at your child's ability to observe and wonder at the tiniest details. Fours are contemplative persons for whom the wonders of God's creation hold delight, awe, and mystery.

Be sure to take time to enjoy the whimsical poem about pets on the *Read to Me* page. You've probably already discovered that your four-year-old has a delightful sense of humor. Help him or her to enjoy the fun in this poem.

Animal Snacks

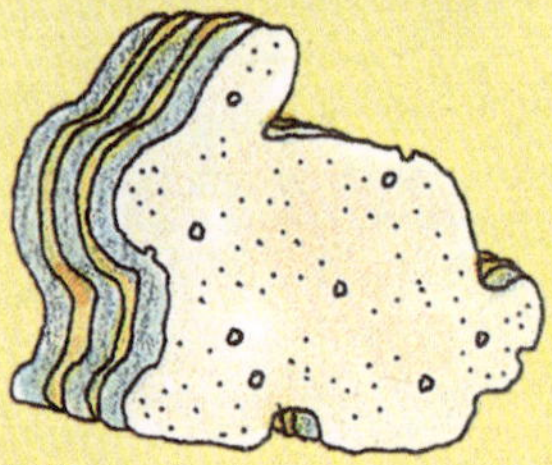

Make a variety of "animal" sandwiches with your child. You will need a sandwich spread, three slices of bread for each sandwich, and a variety of animal-shaped cookie cutters. Cut three of each animal shape to make a sandwich. Spread the sandwich filling on two of the shapes. Stack them and top with the third piece of bread. Serve by standing the animal sandwiches in an upright position on a tray surrounded with pieces of lettuce or spinach.

Animal Friends

(*To the tune of "London Bridge"*)

God made all our animal friends,
Animal friends,
Animal friends.
God made all our animal friends.
God, we thank you.

Lesson 13
God's Gift of Light

The sun is shining.
Our world is warm and bright.

Tell a story about the things you like to do when the sun shines.

God made the sun for us.

Tell a story about the things you like to do when our world is dark.

The sun and the moon are God's gifts to us. God made the sun and moon and stars for us.

Cut out and hang the pictures.

We pray.

How wonderful you are, dear God.
We thank you for your gift of light.
Amen.

Read to Me

Our World is Bright

God gives us the sun
To shine in the day.
It makes us feel warm
When we jump and play.

God gives us the moon
To shine in the night.
It glows in the dark
With lovely, bright light.

God gives us the stars
That twinkle at night.
They wink at us, too,
And make the sky bright.

We thank you, dear God,
For your gift of light.
It helps us to grow
And makes our world bright.

How do you feel in the warm sun?

What do you like best about the daytime?

What do you like best about the nighttime?

Parenting your 4-Year-Old

Sun, Moon, and Stars

Four-year-olds are fascinated by the heavens and by what may lie beyond the world they know. The sky itself is a symbol for heaven, the state of being in joyful union with God forever. The sun determines the coming of each season of the year and, indeed, helps us to count the hours of the day. The moon helps us distinguish one month from another, and the stars have been the compass of navigators for thousands of years.

> When God calls to the stars, they answer, "'Here we are!' shining with joy for their Maker."
> Baruch 3:35

Try to acquaint your child, as best you can in your own environment, with the mysteries of the skies. Perhaps a nearby park or garden has a sundial. On a sunny day, trace the shadow as it falls and see if it tells you the time of day. Follow the various phases of the moon as it grows from a slender "fingernail" to a round silver full moon. Some calendars and clocks will predict these phases. Match the prediction with the real thing!

The stars, of course, are more difficult to see unless you live in a rural area. It may be worth a nighttime drive into the country on a clear night, just to see a canopy of stars. In a large city, a planetarium is usually available to the public in which "star shows" are offered for children and families. Some families have made astronomy a family hobby, and a telescope is taken along on family drives and outings. And there are always children's books on this popular subject!

Above all, help your child experience the rhythm of the day as marked by sun and moon. You might like to make a point one Saturday or Sunday of waking up just before dawn to watch the sunrise. At sunset, notice the reds, pinks, blues, and yellows as the bright sun gives way to moonlight and starlight. Darkness and rest are also gifts from God.

At Home with Your Family

Lesson 13 concludes the children's exploration of God's gifts of creation with a study of the gift of light. They learned to discern and appreciate the different things that happen when the sun is shining and when the world is in darkness.

This lesson on light and darkness also provides early learning experiences that can be built upon for later liturgical understanding of these two great natural gifts. For example, the use of candles in church symbolizes the light of Christ shining in the darkness.

Invite your child to tell you about the illustration on the mobile. You might also listen carefully to see if your child has any negative feelings about darkness. Sometimes it helps to point out, if your child is afraid of the dark, that the moon and stars God made are with us at night. You may want to put a night-light in your child's room for comfort until your child is comfortable with the dark. Remind your child that darkness is a gift from God to help our bodies get the rest they need.

Sun Sandwiches

To make a sun sandwich with your child, cut two pieces of white bread into large circles. Spread pimento cheese or other sandwich spreads on both pieces and place together. Use olives, pickles or pimento pieces for features so that you can create a smiling face on the sun. Cut a square slice of cheese into four triangles. Place them on the edge of the "sun" to serve as rays. Serve with orange juice.

Night Light

(*To the tune of "Twinkle, Twinkle, Little Star"*)

God gave us the sun for day.
We can work and we can play.
God gave us the moon for night,
Shining with a silver light.
God gave us the stars at night,
Twinkle, twinkle, very bright!

(*For second verse, sing the traditional song.*)

Lesson 14
Advent

What a long time we have to wait for Christmas!
We call our waiting time Advent.
We are getting ready to celebrate Jesus' birthday.
Jesus is God's best gift to us.
Color these decorations while you wait for Christmas.

During Advent, we try to be kind and to love others as Jesus did.
While you are waiting for Christmas, you can make an Advent wreath.
Paste the flames on these candles.
Remember that the light of Jesus is with us always.

We pray.

Dear God, help us to be kind and to love others while we wait to celebrate Jesus' birthday. Amen.

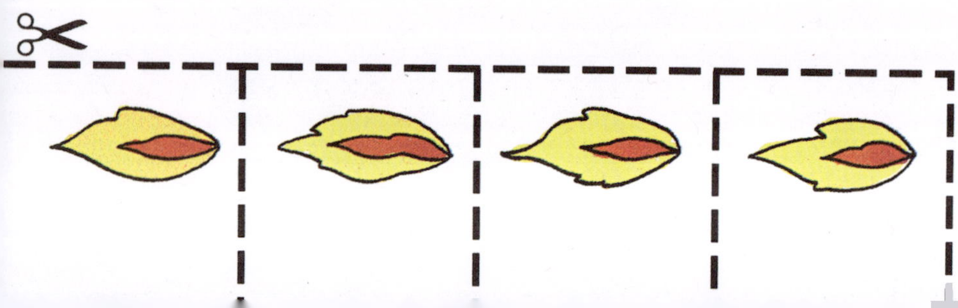

Read to Me

Getting Ready for Christmas

"What's the matter, Lorrie? You don't look happy." Lorrie's mother sat down on the sofa and put her arm around Lorrie. "We're going to unpack all our special boxes and start getting ready for Christmas."

"I don't like waiting for Christmas! Why can't we have Christmas right now?" Lorrie grumbled.

Lorrie's mother explained, "I know it seems like a long time to wait, Lorrie. Before Christmas comes, we celebrate four weeks of Advent, and that *is* a long time."

"But why do we have Advent?" Lorrie asked.

Lorrie's mother answered, "Well, honey, during Advent we do special things to get ready so that we can have a wonderful birthday celebration for Jesus on Christmas Day.

"Let's start now to make our Advent wreath. We'll light one of these candles each Sunday to remind us to get ready to celebrate Jesus' birthday on Christmas!"

What are you going to do to get ready to celebrate Jesus' birthday?

Parenting your 4-Year-Old

When Will Christmas Come?

Advent is the time of preparation for Christmas. During these four weeks, the Church helps us to prepare our hearts for the celebration of the feast of Christmas. Christmas is not only a celebration of the incarnation—the physical birth of Jesus, the Son of God, into our world. It is also a reminder that Jesus will come again at the end of time to bring his kingdom to completion.

For four-year-olds, as for all of us, Advent is the time for getting ready—getting ready to celebrate the birth of Jesus. The emphasis upon Jesus as an infant is inescapable at this time of year. Try to remind your child from time to time that Jesus, like all of us, was born, grew up, died and rose from the dead, and now he is with us always in our hearts.

> Jesus said, "I am the light of the world."
> *John 8:12*

Whenever the feast of Christmas is celebrated, the Church "remembers" the birth of Jesus not only in an ordinary sense but in a special liturgical sense: The event becomes somehow present to us. Jesus is born, not historically again, but in our hearts. We sing in "We Remember" by Marty Haugen:

We remember how you loved us
to your death,
and still we celebrate, for you
are with us here;
And we believe that we will see
you when you come
in your glory, Lord.
We remember, we celebrate,
we believe.*

This remembering, celebrating, believing, and living the mystery of Jesus Christ among us is the true spirit of Christmas.

At Home with Your Family

This Advent lesson acknowledges the anticipation your child is experiencing as he or she waits for Christmas Day. It is important to emphasize traditional religious symbols in your Christmas decorations.

For your four-year-old, waiting to celebrate his or her birthday is a very real experience. Advent can be explained as our time of preparing to celebrate Jesus' birthday at Christmas.

You may wish to introduce the ancient Christian tradition of the Advent wreath. Your child is aware that lighting candles is a special part of our birthday celebrations and can begin to enjoy the lighting of an additional candle each week on the Advent wreath. This is a beautiful symbol of Jesus' coming as the light of the world. As you light the Advent candles, pray together a brief prayer such as, "Jesus, thank you for being with us always. Amen."

A Special Advent Wreath

You may wish to help your child prepare for Christmas by making a special Advent wreath. Help your child cut out the center of a large white paper plate to use for the frame of the wreath. You will need to use green play dough for this activity. Have your child roll a ball of the dough into a long snake. Curve the snake around to form a circle by connecting the ends. Place the playdough circle on the frame and slightly flatten it. Then have your child press four birthday candles into the dough at equal distances. Finally, decorate between the candles with sprigs of evergreen.

Jesus Is Our Light

(*To the tune of "Go 'Round the Village"*)

We light an Advent candle,
We light an Advent candle,
We light an Advent candle
To wait for Christmas Day.

For Jesus' light is shining,
For Jesus' light is shining,
For Jesus' light is shining
Within our hearts today.

UNIT 3

God's Gift of Ourselves

Parenting your 4-Year-Old

Growing and Changing

This season of the year, winter-into-spring, seems to parallel the changeable nature of the four-year-old in the middle of the year. As your child approaches four-and-a-half, you may be surprised to discover that your easygoing four has developed a more demanding attitude. Many children of this age want what they want when they want it, regardless of place, time, or availability.

It is good to remember that growth, like spring, does not come all at once. A bright sunny day may be followed by cold blustery winds or, in some places, a snowstorm. The laws of nature's growth are gradual: one step at a time, and even a few steps backward!

A four's assertion of independence and the ability to make known choices and preferences is a step forward—in a demanding disguise! Tempting as it may be to try to stop negative behavior with the promise of a toy or reward, resist. As your child tests independence to the limit, stay calm and set firm, reasonable boundaries. Reward good behavior with praise and attention. Plan ahead. Bring books and a few small toys to the doctor's waiting room. Involve your child in choosing items for the grocery cart. Boredom is never easy for anyone, especially for a four-year-old!

> Saint Paul wrote, "I planted. . . but God caused the growth."
>
> *1 Corinthians 3:6*

At this time of year, the Church, too, reminds us that the seasons of human life are changeable seasons of growth. As the Church invites us to enter the season of Lent, we are also invited to take a few steps back to look at our beliefs and behavior. What is growing well in our lives? Plant more of those seeds! What is not doing so well? Perhaps that area of life needs more time and attention, and perhaps a little weeding!

As Lent and Easter recall the sacrament of Baptism, think back to the day you brought an infant to the baptismal font and asked that the gift of faith be given to your child. During these next few lessons, celebrate your child's growth and change. Spend a few moments "stepping back" to celebrate your own. In the difficult moments, remember: change and growth, like spring, come only one day at a time!

Additional Parenting Resources

Berends, Polly B. *Whole Child/Whole Parent.* New York: Harper Collins, 1997.

Brazelton, T. Berry, M.D. *To Listen to a Child.* Reading, MA: Addison Wesley, 1986.

Ghezzi, Bert. *Guiltless Catholic Parenting From A to Y.* Ann Arbor, MI: Servant Publications, 1995.

At Home with Your Family

The goal for Unit 3, "God's Gift of Ourselves," is to deepen your child's appreciation of how wonderfully made by God each of us is. The uniqueness and specialness of your child will be affirmed and celebrated. Of all the wonderful gifts God has made in creation, people are the greatest. Through Baptism we become God's own children.

During these five lessons your child will be encouraged to discover and appreciate his or her physical abilities, five senses, and wonderful mental abilities of remembering and imagining. Learning that the ability to feel is given us by God will be part of the unit also. How to respond to and appropriately handle our feelings will also be explored.

Each week as your child brings home the new *Activity Pages*, please find time to affirm his or her special qualities and abilities. Like a young plant in spring, your child's emerging self-identity and sense of self-worth will be enhanced by your care and attention.

For Storytime During Unit Three

Briggs, Raymond. *The Snowman.* New York: Random House, 1978.

Brown, Margaret Wise. *The Runaway Bunny.* New York: Harper Collins Children's Books, 1977.

Brown, Margaret Wise. *Goodnight Moon.* New York: Harper Collins, 1991.

Carle, Eric. *The Very Hungry Caterpillar.* New York: Putnam Publishing Group, 1969.

Clifton, Lucille. *The Boy Who Didn't Believe in Spring.* New York: Viking Children's Books, 1990.

Gibbons, Gail. *Valentine's Day.* Pine Plains, NY: Live Oak Media, 1990.

Lionni, Leo. *Inch by Inch.* New York: William Morrow & Co., 1994.

Ross, Dave. *A Book of Hugs.* New York: Harper Collins, 1983.

Lesson 17
God's Gift of Life

In the Bible we read that
God made the earth and the sky.
God made the sun and the moon and the stars.
God made our wonderful birds and animals and plants.
Can you guess what is the greatest of everything God made?
People are the greatest of all that God made!
God made you.
Draw yourself in God's world.

(fold)

God made millions and millions of people.
But God made only one person like you.
No one else is exactly like you!
God made you and loves you
just the way you are.

Tell what is special about you.

Learn this prayer to pray at home.

We pray.

How wonderful is God!
Thank you, God, for making me.
Thank you, God, for loving me. Amen.

Read to Me

Take Good Care of Yourself

God wants you and all of his children to be healthy and happy.

Here are some things you can do to take good care of yourself.

1. Eat things that are good for you. What foods help you to grow and be healthy?
2. Get some exercise every day. What is your favorite way to get some exercise?
3. Stay together with your friends. Who plays or walks with you?
4. Only go with people you know. Why is this a good rule?

Does your family have other safety rules?

Talk about them with your family at home.

Parenting your 4-Year-Old

Birthday Time!

Will your four-year-old be turning five soon? Are you planning a party? A birthday party and a special birthday cake mark growth and change. These time-honored customs tell the ones we love: "You are special. We're so glad God brought you into the world!"

In planning a party for four-year-olds, remember that, for some children, the need for independence and individual choice may at times override the desire to go along with the group. A game planned for the group may meet with a firm refusal on the part of one or more children. (Some resistance may also be due to shyness or fear of failure.) Perhaps the birthday person will be the first to run off! Be sure to provide alternate activities. Children who may not want to play games will eagerly help put together a special puzzle or do a craft activity. Make sure other adults are available to help with these other games and activities.

> "I praise you, so wonderfully you made me."
> *Psalm 139:14*

A spacious area may invite children to run and chase one another. To discourage this, try to strike a balance between too little space and too much.

If your party is at home, you may wish to set limits in regard to where the guests may go. Be sure to point out the way to the bathroom. Fours should sit at the table during the refreshments. A shy child may need to be paired with a friend in order to be put at ease. It is generally a good idea to serve refreshments near the end of the party.

Fours love party favors. Wrapped surprises "just for coming" are much appreciated, as is a goodie bag for each child to take home.

How many guests to invite? One rule of thumb suggests no more guests than the child's age. A four-turning-five would invite five guests. A birthday party for children this age should last no more than two hours. As the children are leaving, be prepared to hear, "This was the best party!"

At Home with Your Family

The goal in Lesson 17 is to affirm and encourage your child's emerging sense of self-worth. During this lesson, the children were encouraged to see themselves as the greatest of all the wonders God has created for us. Such affirmation and acceptance can help your four-year-old confidently find his or her place in a widening world of peers and siblings.

Your four-year-old's sense of wonder and awe was enhanced by helping him or her to realize that of all the millions of people created by God, only *one* person was made exactly like him or her. This uniqueness reflects God's glory, for, as the Church teaches, "The dignity of the human person is rooted in his creation in the image and likeness of God" (*Catechism,* 1700).

Your child was encouraged to thank God by praying a brief prayer illustrated on the *Activity Page.* Try to pray with your child at home.

Also in this lesson, your son or daughter was encouraged to take care of the beautiful child God made by learning and following some health and safety rules. You may wish to spend some time reading together the list on the *Read to Me* page to be sure that these elements of personal health and safety are understood. Are there other rules you feel would be helpful to add at this time?

A People Collage

Help your child cut or tear from magazines pictures of people who represent a variety of ages and ethnic groups. Help your child to arrange and paste them on a large piece of white paper. Stress that people are God's greatest gifts, no matter how we differ. God has no favorites. God loves each person. Print on the bottom of the picture-collage the words, "God's Greatest Gifts." Tape to a wall in your child's room.

I Am Special

(*To the tune of "Did You Ever See a Lassie?"*)

Here I am, and I am special,
I'm special, I'm special.
Here I am, and I am special—
There's no one like me!

I can look into the mirror,
The mirror, the mirror.
I can see that I am special—
There's no one like me!

UNIT 4
Growing as God's Family

Parenting your 4-Year-Old

The Emerging Person

As you look back at your preschool child's first years, you might label them with three words: exciting, exhausting, and educational. The root meaning of *education* is to educe, to lead forth, to draw out what is already there. By educating your child in life itself, you have led forth and drawn out the best in your son or daughter. You have taught your child so much! And, in many ways, your child has been your teacher, too.

Looking at the four-turning-five, what do we see? We see a child who can most probably wash face and hands, brush teeth, hang up clothing, get into and out of car seats, and in general take an independent stance toward everyday life while asking for help as needed. Listening to the four-turning-five, what do we hear? If teachers and parents have done their work well, we hear the vocabulary, opinions, requests, and affirmations of a real person. A conversation with this real person is a genuine exploration, complete with reasonable responses. It is conversation with a person holding a definite point of view, standing upon a firm foundation built upon earlier verbalizations that were listened to and respected by mom and dad, even when they were not fully understood!

> "It is not the will of your heavenly Father that one of these little ones be lost."
>
> *Matthew 18:14*

The five-year-old desperately wants to use these new skills in ways that please you. In turn, your child wants to know that he or she *is* pleasing you and is doing what you expect. Your praise is a prime motivator. This is a wonderful time to introduce even more new learning into your child's life because the foundational skills to support it are firmly in place. This new learning can of course include new ideas and interests, books and videos, but it can also mean new social skills such as shaking hands when meeting someone or celebrating with others in church on Sunday.

As fours turn five, you will find that your influence is a primary catalyst for growth. You will find that, because you have consistently met your child's needs, your five-year-old will begin to notice and to meet your needs—for a loving pat when you are sad, for companionship, for a good laugh over a joke. Your child will begin to see you as a real person and not simply as "the mom or dad who is there for *me*." These times of mutual recognition, welcome as they are, can also be a quiet shock: "My baby is growing up!" But now is the time to rejoice. You have brought a real person into the world.

Additional Parenting Resources

Nelson, Gertrud Mueller. *To Dance with God: Family Ritual and Community Celebration.* New York/Mahwah: Paulist Press, 1986.

St. James, Elaine. *Simplify Your Life with Kids: 100 Ways to Make Family Life Easier and More Fun.* Kansas City: Andrews McMeel Publishing, 1997.

Yeager, Mark. *Breakfast Is Only the Beginning: A Fun-Filled, Practical Guide for Keeping Up with Your Preschooler.* Minneapolis, MN: Fairview Publishing, 1997.

At Home with Your Family

Unit 4, "Living in God's Family," builds upon your child's deepening sense of wonder and awe at God's goodness and love. The lessons in this unit are planned to help your child appreciate what it means to belong to this special family called the Catholic Church. With Jesus as our model, we try to love God, and others as ourselves.

By nature, four-year-olds are reverent, meditative, and prayerful. In this unit, early learning experiences are provided that will build on these natural abilities to help develop your child's emerging life of prayer. How can you build some experiences of prayer into your family's day?

Early learning lessons that help your child begin to appreciate our great eucharistic celebration are also included in this unit. They will help to establish a foundation for your child's participation in the Mass and the sacraments.

For Storytime During Unit Four

Field, Rachel. Ill. Elizabeth Orton Jones. *A Prayer for a Child.* New York: Macmillan Publishing Co., Inc., 1984.

Hague, Michael. *A Child's Book of Prayers.* New York: Henry Holt & Company Inc., 1998.

Spier, Peter. *Peter Spiers's Rain.* New York: Bantam Doubleday Dell Books for Young Readers, 1997.

Lesson 25

Belonging to a Special Family

Your family loves you very much.

Your family brought you to be baptized. Now you belong to the special family of the Catholic Church.

Color this baby being baptized by the priest. Ask your family who was at your Baptism.

In our special family, the Church,
Jesus shows us how to love one another.
Jesus says, "Love one another
as I love you" (John 15:12).

We learn about Jesus from the Bible.
Here are some stories about Jesus from the Bible.
Tell how Jesus loved people.

Tell these stories about Jesus to
your family.

Jesus fed people who
were hungry.

Jesus helped sick people.

Read to Me

Jesus Loves All Children

Here is a story about Jesus from the Bible. It tells us how much Jesus loves all children.

One day many people came to listen to Jesus. Some of the families brought their children, too. They wanted Jesus to bless their children so they tried to bring the children up close to where Jesus was.

Some of Jesus' friends tried to keep the children away from Jesus. They knew that Jesus was very tired that day. They didn't think Jesus would want to meet the children.

Just then Jesus saw what was happening! He called to all the grown-ups, "Let the children come to me" (Mark 10:14). Jesus knew that children were very important and special.

Jesus hugged each of the little children. He blessed each and every little boy and girl. How happy Jesus and the children were!

Use your imagination. Pretend you were with Jesus and the children.

How did you feel when Jesus hugged you?

Are you glad Jesus loves you? Why?

Parenting your 4-Year-Old

Love's Building Blocks

We human beings learn to love by being loved. The graced truth is that children who have been truly loved pass along to others the love, care, and respect they themselves have received. Love for God is shown by loving concern for others. As the Church teaches, "Love of neighbor is inseparable from love for God" (*Catechism*, 1878).

> "Love one another."
> *John 15:12*

With your help, your four-year-old has already set in place some building blocks in this foundation of love:

Respect for Others A four-year-old has become aware of individuals and their rights. Some fours realize that other people may have feelings and ideas different from their own. A genuine concern for harmony means that minor conflicts can be talked through more easily.

Use of Words A four-year-old has a more secure command of language and can use it to advantage. Language can reflect a new self-control. A four-year-old has also discovered that language can command others. If bossiness seems to be a constant, you may want to remind your four of the little words "please" and "thank you," and remember to speak to your child in a calm and quiet tone of voice.

Your four may also have discovered what are usually called "naughty words" and will try them out on you. At this age, words are just words. Refuse to be shocked.

Emotional Control Because the four can use reason in working out problems, and can put feelings into words, emotions are more balanced. However, in the midst of anger or upset, your four-year-old may say things he or she could not possibly mean or even understand. The truth is, your child is frightened by his or her own anger. If you get angry, you will add to that fright and the child's sense of being out of control.

The building blocks are never perfectly complete, no matter if one is four or forty. Yet it is so true: We begin to learn all we really need to know in life long before we even reach kindergarten!

At Home with Your Family

Lesson 25 is the first of a series of lessons providing beginning experiences for helping your child develop a sense of joy in belonging to the Catholic Church. The lesson began with an explanation that our Baptism marks the beginning of our belonging to this special family. Are there some pictures or mementos of your child's Baptism that you could share with him or her? Such concrete objects and treasured stories can help your child become more aware of and take delight in that great event.

Helping your child come to know and love Jesus as the foundation of his or her developing life of faith was the goal of this lesson. The children were helped to appreciate that from the Bible we learn that Jesus shows us how to love one another. Such awareness, in addition to the Ten Commandments, forms an important basis of our moral activities. From Jesus' kind, thoughtful, loving actions, we can learn to be kind and fair, too.

The story of Jesus and the children was presented here because it is so central to your young child's faith in and love of Jesus. The profound love and respect Jesus showed for each child and his open expression of that love is a treasured part of our Christian tradition that you can read and share again and again with your child. Are there specific ways you can encourage your child to love others as Jesus shows us?

Showing Love Poster

Cut two heart patterns out of white paper. Arrange and paste them in an overlapping, side-by-side position on a piece of red construction paper. Ask your child to draw two pictures, one on each heart, showing how he or she can show love for another. Suggestions: "Help mother set the table"; "Share a toy with a friend."

Jesus Loves Us

(*To the tune of "If You're Happy and You Know It"*)

Jesus loves the little children 'round the world.
(*clap, clap*)
Jesus loves the little children 'round the world.
(*clap, clap*)
Jesus loves us morn and night.
We are special in his sight.
Jesus loves the little children 'round the world.
(*clap, clap*)

Lesson 26
Talking to God

We became God's children at Baptism.
God made us and loves us.
We can talk to God.
We can listen to God.
When we talk and listen to God, we pray.
We can pray to God anytime.
What do you want to say to God when you pray?

Draw yourself with some of God's children.

When we pray we can thank God
for all his gifts.
We can ask God to help us live
as his children.

Color when you will pray to God.
Cut out and wear the button.

Read to Me

Talking to God

When someone gives you a special gift, what do you say? God gives us many gifts.

When we pray, we can say, “Thank you, dear God, for all your gifts.”

God loves us and helps us to love others. When we pray, we can say, “Please help me to be kind and love others, dear God. God bless everyone.”

God asks us to love others and be kind. When we pray, we can say, “I’m sorry, dear God,” if we have not been kind and loving.

God loves us and does wonderful things for us. When we pray, we can say, “How wonderful you are, dear God.”

What is your favorite thing to say to God when you pray?

When is your favorite time to talk and listen to God?

Parenting your 4-Year-Old

Routines

Fours need the security of a daily routine in their lives. They tell time by what is happening to them during the day—breakfast time, preschool time, lunchtime, TV time, bedtime. Each day has a sameness to it that gives the four-year-old good feelings of security. Ask your four-year-old to describe the preschool day. He or she will tell you about the day in the same predictable sequence. Fours need that security both at home and in preschool.

You may want to take time to examine your daily schedule. How does your four fit into your program? Is he or she constantly changing bedtimes and wake-up times? If this is the case, begin slowly to provide a daily sameness for both you and your child. You will find that both of you are calmer and there is a growing harmony in your relationship. Often disruptive behavior in four-year-olds is caused by too little routine in their everyday lives.

> "Pray without ceasing.
> In all circumstances give thanks."
> *1 Thessalonians 5:17–18*

An added benefit to routine is that it can provide more time for fun activities for you and your child. You will also find it easier to have that necessary quiet time in the evening if bedtime is set for the same time each night. It is important to include prayer time as part of the routine you are establishing with your child each evening. Prayers need not be complicated or long. Thanking God for one gift of his love this day and then asking God's blessing on family members can become a treasured ritual. Gradually, the traditional prayers familiar to the family can be added.

At Home with Your Family

Continuing the unit theme of experiencing belonging to our Catholic community, Lesson 26 provides an experience in learning to pray. Your four-year-old is prayerful and contemplative by nature. As you have probably discovered, your child is filled with wonder and awe over the magnificence of God's gifts of creation. That each of us is known and loved by God is also a truth cherished by fours. They are also drawn to simple, reverent rituals of faith. For these reasons, this can be a perfect time to begin to develop your child's life of prayer in response to God's love.

The best and most permanent lessons about prayer are those experiences of praying together that you can include as a natural part of your family life. The example of a prayerful family is a very powerful image that will remain throughout your child's life: "The Christian family is the first place of education in prayer . . . . For young children in particular, daily family prayer is the first witness of the Church's living memory as awakened patiently by the Holy Spirit" (*Catechism*, 2685).

Encourage your four-year-old to pray by talking to God as one talks to a cherished loved one. The *Read to Me* page can help you. It describes the framework for the five kinds of prayer presented here in simple language: blessing and adoration, petition, intercession, thanksgiving, and praise (*Catechism*, 2644). Short, informal prayers in your child's own words are most appropriate. In time, the meanings of our traditional, formal prayers can be explained and understood. You might wish to establish some simple rituals in your home as part of your child's early experiences of faith.

Talking to God

Teach your child this simple litany prayer to emphasize the importance of thanking God for all we have. You are the leader. Teach your child the response.

Leader: My friends bring me such joy and fun.
Response: Thank you, God, for all your gifts to me.
Leader: My family takes such good care of me.
Response: Thank you, God, for all your gifts to me.
Leader: My friends at preschool are fun to play with.
Response: Thank you, God, for all your gifts to me.

My Prayer (*To the tune of "Mary Had a Little Lamb"*)

I am learning how to pray,
How to pray, how to pray.
I am learning how to pray.
I am a child of God.

Jesus, teach us how to pray,
How to pray, how to pray.
Jesus, teach us how to pray
And grow in love each day.

Lesson 27

Coming Together at Mass

Our families come together to pray to
God at Mass.
We all know and love God.
We all pray to God together.

Draw your family going
to Mass together.

We all have our part in the Mass.
We sing songs together. We say prayers together.
We stand and sit or kneel.
We listen when we hear readings from the Bible.

What do we do at Mass?

We pray to God.

We hear about God.

Read to Me

Welcome to Mass!

"Be sure to wear your new red jacket," Carlos' mom said. "You want to look your best today."

"Okay, Mom!" Carlos said. Carlos was excited. St. John's was having a special Mass today for preschoolers and their families. Carlos was going to Mass with his mom, his dad, and his preschool group. He could hardly wait to get to church.

When the family got to the church, there was a big sign on the door. Carlos' dad read it aloud, "Welcome to our preschoolers!" And then the door opened and Carlos' teacher was there, smiling.

"Come right in!" she said. Inside the church, she led Carlos up to the front to sit with his friends from preschool and their families.

Everyone stood to sing. The priest walked to the altar. He said, "Hello! I'm Father Tom. I want to welcome our preschoolers! Welcome to your first Mass together." He prayed the Sign of the Cross as the Mass began.

Have you ever been to Mass with your family? What do people do at Mass?

Did you know any of the other families at Mass?

Parenting your 4-Year-Old

Preparing for Mass

"The parish is the Eucharistic community and the heart of the liturgical life of Christian families; it is a privileged place for the catechesis of children and parents" (*Catechism*, 2226). Many parents wonder about taking their young children to church with them.

Preparation is key, beginning with the parish church itself. It is a wondrous place to a four-year-old. It would be helpful to take your child to church at a time when Mass is not being celebrated. Let your child walk around and ask questions. Talk together about what he or she sees and feels.

> "Let the children come to me."
> *Mark 10:14*

You may wish to show your four-year-old the baptismal font. Tell your child about the day he or she was baptized. Explain that this special day was a very happy occasion for the whole family. The Baptism story will not only help your four feel more at ease in this awesome place. It will also give your child a sense of belonging, since he or she has already been an important part of a happy Catholic celebration.

Explain ahead of time that the time we spend at Mass is the most important time of the week. Even though your child has gone to Mass before, talk about some of the things that will be seen, heard, and experienced at Mass.

Do not expect your child to be a passive watcher the entire time. Try to involve him or her in suitable ways. (To encourage interest, it is best to sit as close to the altar as possible so that the actions there can be seen clearly.) Cardinal Bernardin suggested that parents "should direct children's attention to parts of the Mass that are capable of engaging their attention—various sounds, the offertory procession, the sign of peace."

Try not to become involved in verbal or behavioral tugs-of-war. If your child is a continual distraction to other worshippers, it is best to take him or her to the vestibule or crying room. Emphasize that this is not a punishment but just something needed for now.

At Home with Your Family

An early learning experience explaining the Mass has been provided in Lesson 27. This lesson presented a short description of the first part of the Mass and emphasized that the children are truly welcome at Mass. This theme of welcome is also the theme of the *Read to Me* page. People who are helped to feel welcome at a party or in a group will more happily conform to customs and expectations. Children are no exception. They want to feel welcome and to belong. If going to church is a welcoming experience for them, they will respond positively. One Sunday morning, a toddler marched with his parents into the vestibule of his parish church and began greeting everyone there: "Hi, everybody!" He was happy to be there. He knew he was welcome. He knew he belonged.

As you probably realize, Church norms do not require your child to participate in the eucharistic celebration. However, for four-year-olds, learning to take an active part in the Mass with your family can be a valuable experience of faith. If your preschool group plans a special celebration, suggest that a simple form of the eucharistic prayer be used as found in the *Official Directory of Masses for Children*. The next lesson will help the children to explore the Mass in more detail.

Church Friends

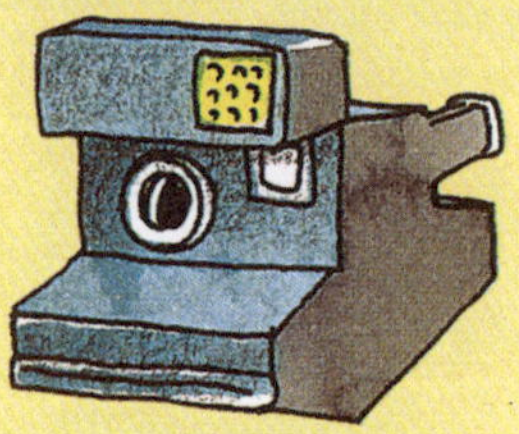

You may wish to arrange to take a picture of your child outside your parish church with the parish priest or his assistant after Mass. You might also arrange with your child's preschool teacher and other volunteers to take pictures of them one day after preschool. Once the pictures have been developed, pick a quiet time at home to talk to your child about the photos. Stress how these people are all part of our special family, the Church. They help us to love God, pray to God, and learn more about God. Reserve the pictures in an envelope or place them in your child's bedroom so he or she can look at them when desired.

Going to Mass

(*To the tune of "Go 'Round the Village"*)

Our families join together.
Our families join together.
Our families join together
At our Sunday Mass.

We sing and pray together.
We sing and pray together.
We sing and pray together
At our Sunday Mass.

Lesson 29

Remembering God

It's summertime!
What do you like to do best in the summer?
Tell these stories about summertime fun.

During the summer we remember how much God our Father loves us.
We remember that we are God's children.
We know we can be happy with God forever.

Make these flags to help you remember how much God loves you.

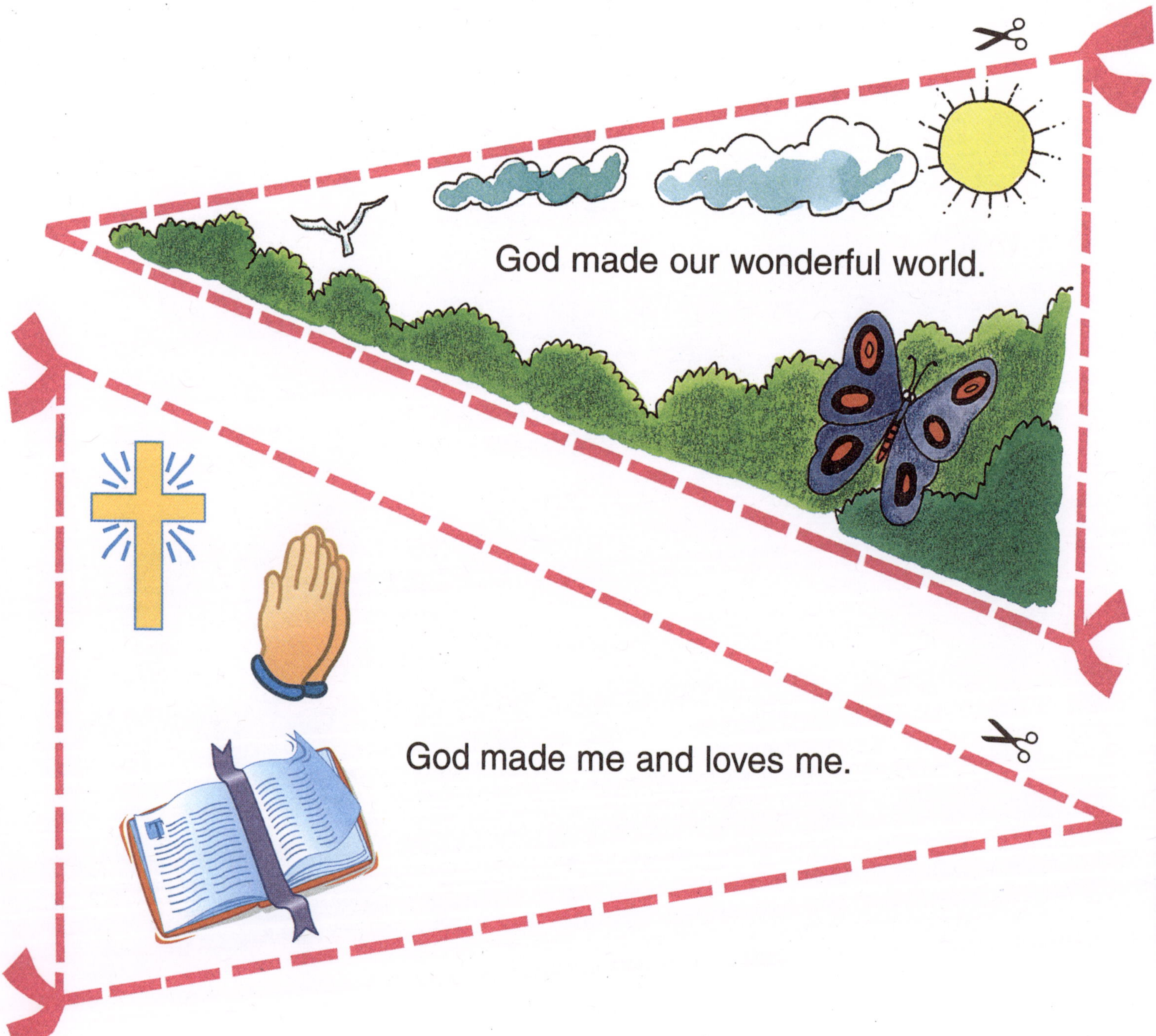

Read to Me

We Remember God

Brenda and her family have fun together in the summer.
Find all the ways they remember God all summer long.

Parenting your 4-Year-Old

Good Old Summertime

For many parents, the lazy and spontaneous days of summer are a fond memory. While summer does bring special freedom, it also makes special demands. For most families, the summer season requires thoughtful planning.

It is sometimes a challenge to maintain the routines established during the school year. Because some changes may need to be introduced during the summer (a new playgroup, perhaps, or a new baby-sitter), it is best to keep familiar routines in place as much as possible.

> "My God will fully supply whatever you need, in accord with his glorious riches in Christ Jesus."
> *Philippians 4:19*

Quiet time is still necessary during the summer. Lunch or supper on a blanket in the yard or at the park, with a few favorite books, puzzles, or tapes carried along, will vary the whole family's pace.

For rainy days, bring out a special "rainy day box" you have prepared ahead of time. You will have filled it with some old clothes and shoes for dress-up, crayons and paper, a few toys saved for this special occasion, and a few books, puzzles, or tapes. The tape of songs accompanying *Discovering God's World* is available for purchase from William H. Sadlier, Inc. (1–800–221–5175 or http://www.sadlier.com). Toys for the box need not be new; anything your child has not seen for awhile will *seem* new. To your child, this box will make a rainy day seem like Christmas!

Be sure to visit your local library for its summer schedule of programs. Farms, museums, and zoos are certainly rewarding places to visit. Just be sure that you do not plan for more time than your child's attention span can handle—perhaps two hours at the most. Planning "down time" is especially important if you are vacationing and touring away from home. No one has fun dragging a tired and cranky preschooler through a long afternoon of sightseeing. This summer, at home or away, resolve to strike a balance between doing and being—and take time to relax!

At Home with Your Family

As your family anticipates the summer season and as this program draws to a close, your child's natural delight in the pleasures of summer will be highlighted. The *Activity Pages* review the great truths of our faith that the children were helped to experience in the program. Invite your child to use the flags to tell you some of the ways God loves each one of us. Can you find a prominent place to display your child's *Activity Page* project?

Remembering God's love and responding to God's love during the summer months was the theme of the maze activity. Are you planning a vacation this summer that you can discuss with your child? How do you anticipate remembering God's love for you and your family on that trip and throughout the summer months?

Perhaps sharing these activities will help your child and your family to be conscious of God's presence through the summer months.

Books for Summer Storytime

Hopkins, Lee Bennett. *Good Books, Good Times!* New York: HarperCollins Children's, 1990.

Jonas, Ann. *Reflections*. New York: Greenwillow Books, 1987.

Goodbye and Hello

(*To the tune of "Goodnight, Ladies"*)

Goodbye, Preschool.
Goodbye, Preschool.
Goodbye, Preschool,
For summertime is here!

Hello, summer!
Hello, summer!
Hello, summer!
It's good to see you here.

(*Continue to the tune of "Merrily We Roll Along"*)

We will play out in the sun,
In the sun, in the sun.
We will play out in the sun,
For summertime is here!

God is with us every day,
Every day, every day.
God is with us every day
And in the nighttime, too.

(*Repeat verses 1 and 2*)

Lesson 30

Mother's Day

Mothers bring us God's gift of life.
Mothers love us and care for us.

On Mother's Day, we can say, "Thank you."
Make a basket full of love to give on Mother's Day.

God loves us and cares for us
through our families.

Draw who loves and cares for you
in the big heart.

Give your basket of love with a big kiss
on Mother's Day.

Father's Day

Fathers bring us God's gift of life, too.
Fathers love us and care for us.

On Father's Day, we can say "Thank you."
What gift would you like to give on Father's Day?
Draw it on this card.

On Father's Day

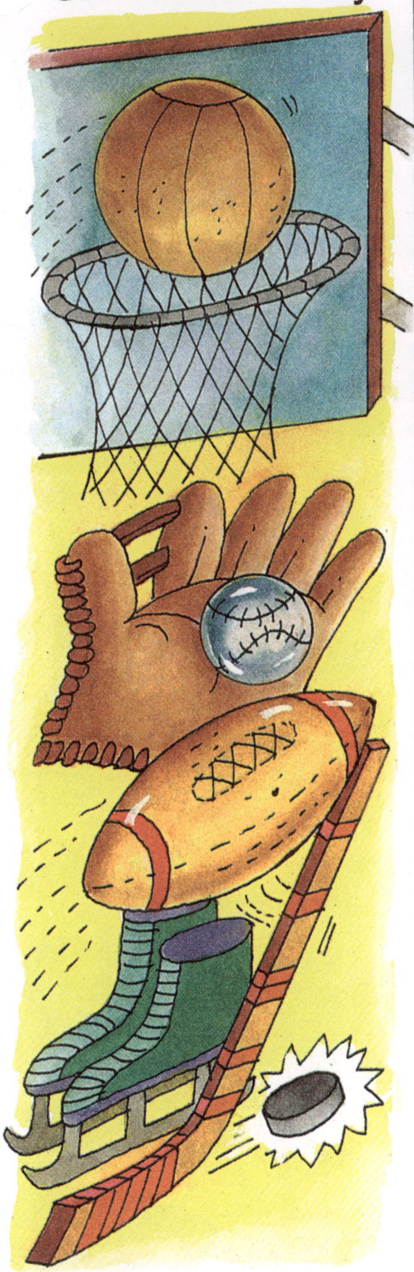

(fold)

(fold)

Thank You

God loves us and cares for us
through our families.

Draw who loves and cares for you
on the card.

Give it with a big hug on Father's Day.

I Love You

From

(fold)

(fold)

Thank You

Lesson 31

Mary Is Our Mother

In the Bible we read that Mary is the mother of Jesus. Mary is our mother, too. Mary loved God always. Mary always said yes to God.

Tell some stories you know about Mary and Joseph. Use the puppets to help you.

Mary, the mother of Jesus, is our mother, too.
Mary loves us and watches over us.

We can pray to Mary.
We can ask Mary to help us live
as children of God.

Lesson 32

Happy Birthday

Today is your special day! Hooray!
How old are you today?
What is your favorite thing to do on your birthday?

Decorate the birthday crown to wear
on your special day.

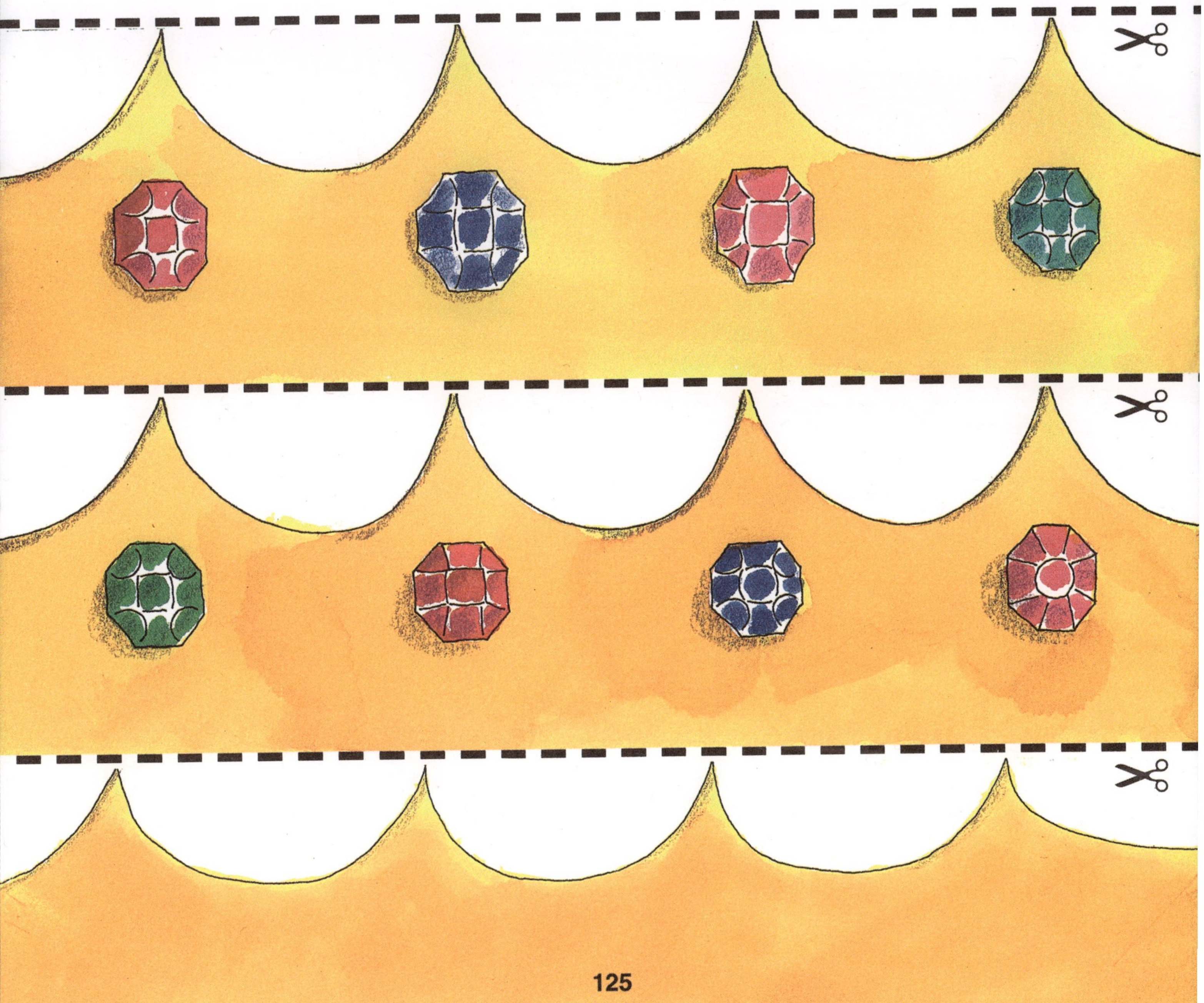

God gives us the gift of life through our mothers and fathers.
On our birthdays we say "thank you" to God for the gift of life.

Cut out the birthday crown.
Wear it to celebrate your special day.

CONGRATULATIONS

____

(child's name)

You are wonderful!

You have completed

____

(program name)

____________	______________________
(date)	(teacher's/catechist's name)
____________	______________________
(date)	(principal's/director's name)

____

____
(child's name)

We are so proud of you!
We all love you!
We are so happy to be
your preschool friends.